ENFP: Understanding &
Relating with the Champion
MBTI Personality Types Series

By: Clayton Geoffreys

Table of Contents

Foreword

Have you ever been curious about why you behave certain ways? Well I know I have always pondered this question. When I first learned about psychology in high school, I immediately was hooked. Learning about the inner workings of the human mind fascinated me. Human beings are some of the most impressive species to ever walk on this earth. Over the years, one thing I've learned from my life experiences is that having a high degree of self-awareness is critical to get to where you want to go in life and to achieve what you want to accomplish. A person who is not self-aware is a person who lives life blindly, accepting what some label as fate. I began intensely studying psychology to better understand myself, and through my journey, I discovered the Myers Brigg Type Indicator (MBTI), a popular personality test that distinguishes between sixteen types of individuals. I hope to cover some of the most prevalent personality types of the MBTI test and share my findings with you through a series of books. Rather than just reading this for the sake of reading it though, I want you to reflect on the information that will be shared with you. Hopefully from reading *ENFP: Understanding & Relating with the Champion,* I can pass along some of the abundance of information I have learned about ENFPs in general, how they view the world, as well as their greatest strengths and weaknesses. Thank you for purchasing my book. Hope you enjoy and if you do, please do not forget to leave a review! Also, check out my website at claytongeoffreys.com to join my exclusive list where I let you know about my latest books. To thank you for your purchase, you can go to my site to download a free copy of *33 Life Lessons: Success Principles, Career Advice & Habits of Successful People*. In the book, you'll learn from some of the greatest thought leaders of different industries on what it takes to become successful and how to live a great life.

Cheers,

Clayton Geoffreys

An Introduction to MBTI

Do you catch yourself trying to understand why others behave the way they do? Have you ever wondered why you act a certain way?

Fortunately, many personality tests today help facilitate that understanding. One of the most commonly used is the Myers-Briggs Type Indicator (MBTI) test. It was developed by Katherine Cook Briggs and her daughter Isabel Briggs-Myers during World War II, as means to determine jobs most fitting for women who desired to contribute to their country. However, it has become so instrumental that it is widely used today. You have probably taken the MBTI at a job interview or if you wanted to work with a psychologist or a life coach on your personal development.

The basic assumption behind the MBTI is that we can determine our preferences through the way we interpret things. These preferences are cornerstones of our values, needs and motives.

So how was the Myers-Briggs Type Indicator (MBTI) typology created? This test expands Carl Gustav Jung's theory presented in his work *Psychological Types*, which divides types of personality into eight basic categories. The division in Jung's theory takes into account one dominant cognitive function and combines it with introvert/extrovert distinction. MBTI is much closer to everyday life. An average person rarely uses only one function. They rely on secondary functions as well. One dimension was also added to show whether a person is more of an intuitive or a rational type.

People are different due to the four main psychological dimensions, which Myers and Briggs call preferences:

Attitudes (Extroversion/Introversion)

How we gather information (Sensing/Intuition)

How we process information (Thinking/Feeling)

Lifestyle (Judging/Perceiving)

By combining these four dimensions we come up to sixteen types of characters coded by four letters.

Users' feedback shows that MBTI really brings new knowledge about oneself, and about the way we truly are. It helps us realize our weak points, our strengths, what fits us and what does not and that way, we can fine-tune our life to our abilities.

The Four Dimensions of the MBTI

The Myers-Briggs Type Indicator is based on a distinction which is four dimensional; each of the dimensions has two poles. You will find out which type you are, depending on the score you obtained in each dichotomy.

Of course, the Myers-Briggs Type Indicator (MBTI) is not perfect, but neither is any other test. Each of us is carrying something from both sides of the dichotomy. We must take into account that behavior differs in various situations, but there is a tendency to lean towards one of the poles.

The dimensions of the MBTI are these:

1. Extroversion (E) vs. Introversion (I)

Introverts are more oriented towards inner life. They usually have a few friends, but respect them more than extroverts. They get their energy from the time spent in solitude. Interaction with others can even be unpleasant, and they prefer to listen to the conversation rather than to engage in it. On the other hand, extroverts are friendly, open, communicative and often impulsive. They get the energy from social contacts and are oriented towards outside. They enjoy talking and are comfortable with expressing their feelings and attitudes.

2. Sensing (S) vs. Intuition (N)

Sensing types are oriented towards the present. They pay attention to details and believe in what they can touch. They prefer facts and what is in front of them. Intuitive types are primarily concentrated on the past or future, trying to grasp the total experience. They give advantage to thoughts, abstract theory and fantasy. They always seek new and better ways to do things.

3. Thinking (T) vs. Feeling (F)

Thinking types have better understanding of logical principles, and easily operate with factual knowledge. They are not prone to compromises. They prefer dealing with facts and numbers rather than with people and can be considered as ruthless. The Feeling types, however, are better at emotions and empathy. They accept compromises, and love to make people around them feel good.

4. Judging (J) vs. Perceiving (P)

Those with a preference for judging come with the love for order, plans, rules and reliability. Preference for perceiving (P) brings great capacity for improvisation, and work wonders without harmonograms, with all our options wide open.

Why is the Myers-Briggs Type Indicator Significant?

Myers-Briggs Type Indicator (MBTI) is probably among the most frequently used personality tests in the world. Roughly, 2 million people take it every year. It is used mostly in HR departments, but you can meet with it in marriage and career counseling, wherever groups or teams of people need to get along with each other.

What we determine from personality types is meant to better personal and professional relationships. Motivation, management, communication, social relations – all of these are far more successful when you have a better understanding of yourself and people you are working with. You learn how to treat individuals with great care, respect, and appreciation through learning about the types of characters. In business, evaluation of character should be used only to determine which work place would be most suitable for a specific employee.

Understanding different types of character also help us predict the way in which a person will act in various situations, how they make their decisions, and what they will focus on etc. For example, a person with a strong Judging preference (J) will be extremely nervous if he or she goes on a trip with their family without all of the details meticulously taken care of. There are many ways to solve problems. So, different personality types can come to the same solution taking different paths. It is not a question of determining the right way from the wrong one, but a question of understanding how our minds work and respect others' individuality.

On the other hand, some types of characters are, indeed, better at certain professions. Many professional teams could be more successful if members would understand their colleagues' way of thinking. Unfortunately, an employee can have a bad opinion of a coworker only because he gets to the same solution using different methods. That is why MBTI is essential for most companies.

To find out your character type and to accept your weaknesses and strengths is a part of a healthy self. The worst thing we can do to a child is to criticize his or her character. For example, if both parents are a Judging (J) type of a character and they have a Perceiving (P) son, they might not be able to understand his creative expression. A Perceiving child usually has no sense of order which, on the other hand, the judging personality, has enormous need for – and, therefore will not be able to understand the witty expressionism of the child. Being misunderstood during childhood can affect their self-esteem in the worst possible way.

Again, why is the Myers-Briggs Type Indicator (MBTI) significant? Firstly, it can help us understand our own flaws and assets. Secondly, we can learn to appreciate others' uniqueness, and profoundly connect to different types of people that we might readily dismiss in other circumstances. We can learn what we are looking for in a partner, a friend, or what kind of work is fit for our personality type, hence leading a more fulfilling and rewarding life.

Uncovering the "Champions": Who is an ENFP?

ENFP is an acronym for Extroverted Intuitive Feeling Perceiving, which tells us what combination of eight possible poles is typical for these personalities:

Extroversion – dominant, determined, focused on the outside world

Intuition – innovative, visionary, focused on the future

Feeling – caring, generous, empathic

Perceiving – spontaneous, inconsistent, adaptable

If you are an ENFP, you belong to 3-5% of the population with these traits. However, the influence of this small percentage of people is great, since the effect an ENFP has on others is enormous. In a nutshell, ENFPs are enthusiasts, idealist and creators.

14

The most prominent characteristic of this personality type is inexhaustible optimism. If you are an ENFP, your optimism is so strong, that you are genuinely astonished when things do not go the way you had expected, or people do not behave as you would want them to. Among all of the types, ENFPs are probably most inclined to positive thinking.

As an ENFP you are capable of doing whatever you are interested in – but only what you are interested in. You need to live in accordance with your values. You are free, independent and original to the core. Imitating someone is considered to be an offense to your authenticity.

You are open-minded, with a flexible intellect, and a remarkable range of interests and abilities. There are many ENFPs among artists. This personality type has many options when choosing a profession, but you always pick one you can use to interact with people.

15

If you belong to this type, you have most certainly noticed you get easily excited about new ideas and thoughts, but you may find the details boring. Because of that, you have a tendency to start a lot of projects feverishly, but do not finish them because a new idea comes to your mind. You frequently act on an impulse, and cannot stand routine and repetitive jobs, even more so if that means you would have to stay indoors.

ENFP is a real "people-person". If you are one, you are friendly, open, communicative, and simply love to be noticed. That is why you cope with rejection poorly, even though it is very rare. Out of all types, the "Champion" is a social genius, who loves the crowd, and the crowd loves them. If you see a group of people with one who is making them all laugh, rest assured it is an ENFP. They are unconventional, and if someone is effortlessly persuaded into doing something crazy to entertain the party, that is them. Being an ENFP, you like to comment on others, or tell stories about what had happened last Friday. Still, you know there is more to it. You love quality time with only one significant other with whom you share ideals and a deeper connection. You enjoy fine art of seduction and flirtation.

You might frequently have a problem with keeping attention. You are a bit absent minded, loosing stuff and forgetting about things constantly. You might even have a problem staying focused when listening to long lectures and speeches. This is a consequence of your mild hyperactivity, and your need to seek thrills and experiments. It is possible that you overlook illnesses until the symptoms become impossible to ignore.

The analysis of cognitive functions shows that an ENFP has:

- Dominant: Extroverted Intuiting (Ne) - This means you have ability to interpret situations and see their connections to other situations and principles.

17

- Auxiliary: Introverted Feeling (Fi) - This is shown through ENFP's firm system of values and strong beliefs.
- Tertiary: Extroverted Thinking (Te) – ENFPs are organized, efficient, and systematic.
- Inferior: Introverted Sensing (Si) - This function makes an ENFP recall previous experiences in detail.

The "Champion" is probably the most optimistic person you know-warm, friendly, with many interests and talents, and also with an unyielding system of values.

Why are ENFPs Indispensable Leaders?

There are many ways to lead a group of people or team. Some tend to be strict, focusing on the work that needs to be done. While others are quiet controlling and only appear to give a final judgment. Then there are those loved, followed by the ones hated by those they lead. This does not apply only to work. We can say the same when it comes to a holiday with family, a school project, volunteering actions or taking care about a household.

There are people, who are natural born leaders; who are always appointed to be the team leaders. This person is, as a rule, an ENFP personality type. He or she is loved by the people, and if a group has an opportunity to pick their superior, it will most probably be someone belonging to this type. If you are an ENFP, you need to know that this is because you have immense enthusiasm that is contagious to everyone around you. You are an inspiration to the team you lead. Enormous amount of energy flows around you, and only a few can resist immersing themselves into a shared project.

You get easily excited about new ideas, and you are constantly looking for a better way of doing things. This is why your teammates feel at ease pitching new thoughts and presenting innovative methods and solutions to a problem. Your leadership style can be described as democratic and flexible. You are innovative, and in fact, you probably openly hate rules just for the sake of them being rules. You are not afraid of testing your team's brave strategies, and for that, you are a respected leader. You are the one that makes your teammates eager to work.

Since one of the most important things for an ENFP is helping others grow, this adds to the fact that you are an indispensable leader. Not only do team members share your passion for a project, but you also help develop their personal assets. If you had an opportunity to lead the team, you probably noticed how interested you were for your people's prosperity and both personal and professional improvement. You can become so interested that, unfortunately, it becomes more important than the actual work. You take into account their personal problems, you know which one of them had an argument at home; you are aware of their aspirations and plans. Furthermore, you care to motivate them into being the best they can possibly be. To someone else, this would be too draining. Yet for you, it is probably the best part of the leading role. You love developing one's potential and seeing them flourish in front of you.

Although your subordinates usually like you for your "humanistic" approach to work, that same personality trait means that you might neglect the project itself, some details, deadlines, or financial/technical limitations of a proposed solution. To some other personality types, mainly those with predominant Judging (J) preference, this can cause a great amount of stress and dissatisfaction.

ENFPs are natural born and, in most cases, appreciated leaders. If you work on your planning and organizational skills, your innovative, brave and visionary personality will influence many lives. You will bring both success and personal growth to everyone you lead.

The 7 Greatest Strengths of an ENFP

An Extroverted Intuitive Feeling Perceiving type of personality has various strengths, and most of them become prominent in social interactions. An ENFP is a social type of person, and that is the area of life they shine in. The combination of these strong points makes a "Champion" out of an ENFP:

1. Excellent Verbal Communications Skills

ENFPs have the ability to express themselves in a clear and well-received manner. If you belong to this type of personality, you communicate in a way that attracts people. Your intuitive personality has given you almost supernatural ability to sense what others think and are about to say. Moreover, one has a feeling that you can read minds and your warm nature allows people you are talking to feel as though they are not being scrutinized. Everyone you talk to feels as though you have known each other for ages. You are completely comfortable in expressing your feelings, thoughts and attitudes, and there is little place for misunderstanding when talking to you.

2. Perceptive of Others' Motives

The fact that you are extremely sensitive to the inner life of another person is connected to your communication skills. Due to your intuition and immense capacity for empathy, no thought goes unnoticed by you. You know that this comes naturally to you, but others may be astonished by your understanding of how their mind and souls work. Your inborn sympathetic nature accepts everyone as they are. That, combined with a vast capacity for sensing every little thought in one's mind, makes you an expert in psyche. When talking to an ENFP, we can almost feel as they even see the desires, wishes and reflections hidden from us.

3. Motivating and Inspiring

ENFPs are fantastic motivators of others. Being an ENFP, you always see the best in everyone, and make people see themselves in a positive light, gently pushing them forward. Your enthusiasm is a motivator, by itself, and it breathes life into every idea. People around you feel they can achieve whatever they set their minds on. And it is probably true. Although you see only the good in people, you are not an optimist without a reason. You see what is really there, and you have a way of bringing it out into the light. Your energy pushes people further when they are about to give up.

4. Loving With Intensity

ENFP's grand capacity for love makes them a real treasure for their families and partners. Being an ENFP, you are not afraid to give all you have to someone you love. You value deep relationships, and you are ready to commit yourself completely. Even though you love to flirt and seduce, you are looking for a profound connection with someone you share ideals and principles with. You can move mountains for someone you care about, and it gives you a great satisfaction to make your loved ones happy. You are driven by an urge to fulfill other people's needs, you see ahead of them and do whatever it takes to make them feel adored.

5. Pleasant and Energetic

Most of all personality types, ENFPs are oriented towards other people, and are great company. If you see someone walking into the room and all of a sudden it appears everything is getting a little bit livelier, be sure it was an ENFP that showed up. If you are an ENFP, then you know that you accept everyone the way they are, and you may communicate with almost anybody with the same emotional and social openness. You are, simply, fun to be around. You make people laugh and feel good. If the party is dull, you will turn it around in no time. Your energy is contagious. You love making people feel good and appreciated.

6. Always Settle for Win-Win Situations

As selfless as you are and oriented towards making others satisfied you are more than ready to compromise. You are committed to your goals, but if that collides with a healthy social interaction, you will choose what makes everyone simply - happy. You value pleasant communication and good relations over your own gain. You also avoid any confrontation, so you are willing to give in, just to make everyone content. You are sensitive to any form of criticism, and you are even more reluctant to pass judgment on others. Therefore, negotiating with you is always a congenial affair. Unfortunately, you are sometimes a victim of exploitation by others because of that. In the end, everyone will gladly cooperate with you, and that is why this is an asset for an ENFP.

7. Committed

Wholehearted and energetic, ENFPs can be passionate and committed, both to people and to a cause. Being an ENFP, you do need constant stimulation, and you get bored easily if something is repetitive and segmented. But, if you see the whole picture, and feel strongly about something, you may take it up to yourself to pursue the cause to its fulfillment. This applies to the ideas, and to personal relationships. You will do whatever it takes to make a relationship work, and if you feel an intense connection with someone, you will do your best for your partner.

The 5 Greatest Areas of Improvement for an ENFP

Same as everyone else in the world, ENFPs have both advantages and disadvantages. However, knowing our weak points is the first step in our personal growth. There are far more positive sides in every ENFP's personality, and therefore, weaknesses are best to be considered as areas of improvement:

1. Enthusiasm Curtails Realistic Thinking

Being an ENFP, you are loved and sought for because of your vast enthusiasm. You are a motivator; you are capable of inspiring everyone to achieve their best. Still, your optimism and genuine love for the people make you stop seeing things as they really are. It is wonderful to see the world as if it were filled with good intentions and kind people. It is most certainly advisable to keep a positive attitude and a belief in oneself, but there is a line between a healthy sense of inner locus of control, and the idea that all is, inevitably going to work out just fine. ENFPs need to take off their pink glasses, and see the world for what it really is. That does not mean that you have to become a pessimist (nor that it could ever be achieved), but in order to be prepared for different life situations, in which people do not always behave in the best possible way and things do not always go as planned, it is good for an ENFP to accept the possibility.

2. Resistance to Ending Dysfunctional Relationships

Connected to the previous area of improvement for your personality type is the fact that you may have a tendency to stay in a situation that is not right for you, believing it will turn all right in the end. But at that point, the end is usually far behind you. It is just your belief in people and good luck that keep you from realizing that. Like all ENFPs, you have a wonderful capacity for seeing only the best in everyone, but sometimes you do not see that it is the relationship that is malfunctioning. The reason for staying involved with someone when you are just not right for each other lies in the fact that you consider the failure as your fault, and your responsibility is to fix that. Sometimes, it is simply not so, and it is, unfortunately, a waste of valuable time.

3. Getting Bored Easily

ENFPs get easily fed up with anything that is somewhat repetitive and constant. This is definitely an area of improvement for you if you belong to this personality type, since this can endanger both social relations and work. You might develop a tendency of frequently changing partners - if you do not find that perfect deep connection, you will go and search for it in the next partner. What drives you is a noble desire, but the consequences can be unhealthy. Furthermore, the same trait can cause you to start projects without

31

finishing them, and maybe even switch jobs repeatedly, just to find some stimulus.

4. Extreme Dislike for Criticism

No one likes to be criticized. There is an ideal of taking every criticism as a way to evolve and grow. But it is hard to achieve. If you are an ENFP, it is even harder. You have a trait that is extremely prominent. Even the slightest negative comment, no matter how well it was put is seen as an insult, a direct attack on your personality, and a demonstration of how poorly someone knows you. You either get sad or angry. There is a large area of development for you – if you learn how to see the critique objectively, to take into consideration whether it is justified, and think of it as a guide for a better self. This will build even stronger connections with people with whom you interact. Also, you have to remember, criticism does not necessarily lead to a conflict – another form of interaction you absolutely hate. All of these are to be taken as a way to build a deeper connection. As Erich From wrote, what is valued is the depth of the connection between the two lovers, and not the question of how they get along.

5. Clinginess and Overwhelming

ENFPs have the warmest nature. They are affectionate, and love to talk about their feelings. What is so hard to an INTJ, for example, comes as the most natural thing to an ENFP. Being able to express your feelings, talk about them, show them in every possible situation is what brings you joy and puts a smile on your face. You are loving, passionate, and you would do the impossible to make the object of your affection feel on top of the world. You love to know every detail about what he or she had been doing that day. But, why is this categorized as an area of improvement? Even though this is a trait that many would love for their partner to have, it can be overwhelming for some. Especially Thinkers (T) may find it unpleasant. You, on the other hand, might feel rejected if you expect the same from others. So, it will prevent many misunderstandings if we keep in mind that our need for affection is different from others'.

What Makes an ENFP Happy?

ENFPs are generally very happy people. It does not take them too much to feel good and full of life. They are extremely optimistic, and that trait stays with them through their entire life. Very few things can make them feel depressed or sad. Even if they do feel disheartened because of something, it is short lived. They believe in their capabilities, and know that most of the problems can be resolved if they just put some extra effort into solving them.

If you are an ENFP, what is important for you is to live in harmony with your ideals. You need to be as authentic as one possibly can. And, by doing so, you feel in harmony with yourself, full of liveliness and ready to take over the world. You enjoy exploring yourself, as well as others, and take real pleasure in viewing all the differences of human mind and soul. You can see beauty in everyone and everything. This is a rare quality. It gives you enormous pleasure to help someone flourish, whether it is a client, a coworker, a friend or partner, or just a mere acquaintance.

You love being around people, as much as people love to be in your company. You thrive when you are the center of attention, you love to entertain, and you feel great in the crowd. On the other hand, after the day is over, you still need some solitude time as well, or time spent with your significant other to contemplate on deeper aspects of life. You are in a constant pursuit of your inner harmony and peace, and need a profound connection with your partner, family or with yourself.

ENFPs are oriented towards the future. What is temporary and the past, does not take too much of your energy. You keep their optimism up by looking forward and seeing all those options ahead. You are not much of a planner, but you do enjoy fantasizing about anything that is possible, anything you can accomplish. You are an original thinker, open-minded and independent. You are not afraid of limitless alternatives and inventive ways of thinking. On the contrary, you genuinely enjoy putting risky strategies into practice.

An ENFP gets satisfaction from the first stages of projects or relationships. Being an ENFP, you love new beginnings, and they give you a boost of energy. This can cause you to be unsteady in your work or love life. But every new beginning makes you wake up as a Phoenix. All the ingrown paths that some new venture can walk you down excite you to the core. In general, you feel good in varied situations. This is where your charisma takes over and leads you to success. The uncertainty of these circumstances, and your victorious endeavor, gives you a zest for life.

Flexibility and lack of structure are the best situations for you as an ENFP. You are unfulfilled when confined to plans or rules and you see those as limitations. You are spontaneous and cheerful in their freedom.

Emotional excitement is what makes an ENFP tick. Unlike some other personality types, which have a strong need for stability and would gladly accept something that an ENFP would mark as dull, this personality needs strong and intensive emotional experiences. Combining this strong system of values makes ENFPs intense people with a massive life force and full of vigor.

What are Some Common Careers of an ENFP?

Choosing a right career is one of the few most crucial decisions in life. Depending on one's system of values, it can even be the single most important resolution one has ever made. Confucius said: "Choose a job you love, and you will never have to work a day in your life," and those who are lucky to have done just that, know how right he was.

For an ENFP, doing the job one likes is even more important. They have a strong need to live in accordance with their values, interests and preferences. Being an ENFP, you choose workplaces in which you may interact with lots of people, and simply need to have a stimulating job. It is offensive to an ENFP to ask them to work on an assembly line, or do anything that is not diverse and thought provoking.

39

Similar to ESFPs, ENFPs are very commonly found in arts. Most of all, they are masters of language use, and they love to speak in metaphors, so they are commonly seen among writers, and poets. If you are an ENFP, your intuitive nature and affinity towards strong and deep feelings have made you very perceptive of the human mind – that, combined with the ability to express your profound emotions, makes you a great artist. You may use this to become a very gifted actor as well, and by doing that, you can explore different personalities and be different people yourself – an ultimate diversity of life, one might say.

That same trait enables ENFPs to become great psychologists when they wish to. Using your intuition, you understand people extremely well. You might also relate to anybody, and interact with them on their level, adapting the language, context and content of conversation. You might be an ideal therapist, since you do see inside the people, but you are more concentrated on their potential. You have limitless belief in everyone's ability to prosper and be great. Your egalitarianism gets its real purpose in this line of profession. The warmth of your nature will make clients confide in you, and have faith in your methods.

Being an ENFP, you need constant stimulation and you might be very happy working as a journalist or a reporter. This is actually a kind of work which can keep you occupied and you might be committed to it for long time. A job as a reporter brings you just what you need – meeting new and different people, change of scenery every day, not having to delve on technicalities and bureaucratic questions, not feeling like a big fish inside a small bowl, etc. You can push boundaries, and put all that extra energy to a good cause.

You may also be a very good manager. You, yourself, frequently do not see a project to its end, but on the other hand, you can delegate very well and therefore this position comes natural to you. You know people to the bone, know their abilities and see what they can easily accomplish. You are born to be a leader, and people instinctively look up to you for guidance. ENFPs motivate and encourage everyone around them. This is why you might excel in a position of a manager, or an HR specialist in a company.

ENFPs are sometimes inclined to work for the entertainment industry and they can have a great success in it. This is why they are usually in a spotlight of every party. This line of work has some dangers for an ENFP, though. They can be prone to addictive substances in pursuit of stimulation. Unfortunately, these are rather common and more available in the movies and the world of music.

If you are an ENFP, you might also shine as a politician. You have developed communication skills, you know the values of compromise, and the crowd loves you. Your philanthropy can make a great difference to the world, if you get to the position where decisions are made. Having an ENFP for a leader is considered a real treasure by the people. Barack Obama, for example, is an ENFP type of personality.

ENFP is one of the personality types who have almost all of the options open. Being one, you are very intelligent, multi-talented, and creative. You can fit into almost every social group, and are always welcomed onto a team. Therefore, the choice is yours.

Common Workplace Behaviors of an ENFP

ENFPs need to have a job that fits their interests. When this happens, they can be very dedicated to it. Being an ENFP, you are usually full of ideas, and you bring new perspectives to any project. You are completely dedicated to any new project, but it needs to keep you constantly engaged and stimulated. Otherwise, you get bored and leave it unfinished. This happens in most cases. That is why a good career choice is a must if you are this type of person. Additionally, coworkers should be prepped and ready to take over from where an ENFP has left off, since unfinished projects will keep on coming. Even if you get to the end of the project, the result is frequently somewhat different from how things were supposed to work out. ENFPs are masters of improvisation, so if you are one, you thrive in unexpected circumstances.

When working in a team, you usually take the role of the leader, or of someone who is continuously challenging old ways. Your inputs are generally not made in a practical way, but are important contributions as action initiators and motivators. You are relentlessly trying to find positive traits in every person, the brighter side of every situation and you believe in an optimistic outcome so hard that you tend to overlook even the most obvious shortcomings or irresolvable issues. Every team should use an ENFP member as a source of energy and liveliness.

Since ENFPs are marvellous in every social situation, you are easily adaptable to almost any kind of team. However, because you are a social chameleon, you may have a problem with some work situations. You do not like someone forcing rules upon you or telling everyone what to do. You might be influenced, but only indirectly through your feelings. You thrive when there are no boundaries or strict structure. ENFPs hate being inferior to or dependent on someone's instructions. On the other hand, even though you do not ask, others gladly follow you, look up to you, and search for inspiration and leadership. You are the type of leader that praises your team, glorifies his or her success and makes everyone feel appreciated.

You get along with almost everybody. It is in your nature. Charm is the essential part of your work persona. But, if you do get into a disagreement, or if you are misunderstood, you have a tendency to withdraw from interaction, and become either depressive or vindictive. You need continuous feedback, and preferably a positive one. If coworkers get into quarrel, ENFPs are the ones trying to bridge the disagreement.

You are enthusiastic, original, joyful and able to do whatever you set your mind on. You are best in workplaces where you can cooperate with others – you are great at getting people to agree on something, work together, or persuade them. You are less competent at organizational details, though.

As an ENFP, you need variety. This applies to both work assignments and coworkers. The ideal work setting for you is a position where you could meet a lot of new people, change the environment, advance, and regularly get new assignments and projects. You get edgy expecting some excitement from the job. If it does not come by itself, you are capable of inducing it yourself and waiting for 5 minutes until midnight to finish what is needed.

This personality type acts as a catalyst. Most ENFPs are a helping hand to coworkers to prosper and develop their full potentials. If you are an ENFP, you offer your time to your coworkers so much, that you might, at times, neglect responsibilities. You often find yourself stuck in-between demands of the superiors on one hand and the needs of your subordinates on the other. In this case, you are more inclined to support your team, and you may wear yourself out completely in this way. Sometimes, mostly by your own will, you get so exhausted by work, that you feel as if the job is not giving you any satisfaction. That is why you are supposed to take a break, from time to time, to think over your goals, priorities and needs, and try not to invest so much energy in others.

ENFP: Parenting Style and Values

ENFPs take their parenting role very seriously and they are fully committed to it. On the other hand, they are also very playful. Being an ENFP, you remain in contact with your inner child throughout your entire life, so you love to play with your children and are very good at it. Still, you find it crucial to hand down your values and beliefs to your offspring. This firm system of values provides an environment that is rich in meaningful life lessons to a child. You will relentlessly try to create a positive atmosphere and surrounding that is as close to the ideal place for growing up as possible. You care for your family and bring them warmth and laughter.

Since you are a little bit unstable and impulsive, you may behave that way in the upbringing of your offspring as well. You might be best friends with your child, laugh and run with them at one moment, and then act as a strict authority in the next. This inconsistency is a consequence of an inner conflict of every ENFP parent – wanting to be at your child's level, but at the same time you feel pressured to implement your deeply rooted values. In other words, if you are an ENFP parent, you probably feel the desire to be your children's best friend, but if they act in a way that contrasts with your beliefs, you will probably go back to your role of a mother or a father, and make sure that they understand what the rules are. This can be disorienting and frustrating for your child.

Nevertheless, children of ENFP parents feel loved, because they receive a lot of support and open affection. You appreciate authenticity and believe in being yourself. Thus you provide the same for your child – respecting your child's individuality and allow a lot of space for growth and development. If you are ENFP, rest assured that your children appreciate your loving and warm personality, and a joyful approach to life.

Your enthusiasm can sometimes be a bit overwhelming for a child. This is especially typical of families where a child has preference for thinking (T) or sensing (S), and therefore has a problem to understand their parent's need for public display of love and affection.

If you are an ENFP parent, you are, of course, able to take care of everyday responsibilities, like taking your son to school in the morning, picking him up from a soccer practice, and making him a sandwich. You are also able to punish your kid if he goes directly against your values. However, these aspects of parenting are not your strong point. You have a rich imagination and great creativity, and these qualities bring a whole world of fun, excitement and dynamics to your child's life.

Why Do ENFPs Make Good Friends?

ENFPs are warm, sociable people. They always try to be in harmony with others' opinions and feelings. Energetic as they are, they are very popular and most people love being in their company. All of the preferences (E, N, F, and P) cause them to be real "people persons" and energizers.

Being an ENFP, you are able to connect with nearly every person, no matter how different they may be. You genuinely care about people, and have a lot of understanding for everyone's needs. Optimists to the core, you always see just the good in others, and you are capable of getting the best out of everybody. That makes everyone feel appreciated and accepted. Therefore, as an ENFP, you never lack company. All of us love to be around someone who believes in us!

If you are an ENFP, you probably get great satisfaction from being supportive to others, and you love helping them perfect their skills and become anything they can be. You are appreciated by your friends for your kindness and your warm and giving nature. You are an idealist, and you seek real personal relationships with no deception or superficial interactions. If that is the case, you can be a really great motivator and lead your friends to success in every endeavor.

Although they generally embrace almost every type of person, there can be a problem between ENFPs with a strong F component, that is Feeling, and other personality types with a strong T (Thinking) component. Thinkers usually do not respond favorably to excited cordiality. On the other hand, ENFP has an intuitive understanding for Thinkers "standoffishness", but if that situation happens over and over again, even a warm ENFP can close their heart in this relationship. ENFPs can also feel threatened by a person with strong Judging (J) preference, because they have a tendency of taking every critique personally. This causes them to feel irritated or stressed, because they assume that the negative opinion means disappointment.

ENFPs are good friends to diverse people. Being an ENFP, you do not take into account social or economic status and you may share emotions and interests with all sorts of personalities and individuals with completely different backgrounds. ENFPs are a sort of social chameleons. They fit perfectly into every social setting and people around them feel they have known them for years, even if they had spoken for a couple of minutes.

If you are an ENFP, you probably sought other intuitive temperaments (NF) to be your friends, because of your shared enthusiasm for life. You also appreciate intuitive thinkers (NT). You need authenticity and depth from your close friends and, therefore, you prefer those similar to you - expressive and affectionate.

Of course, even though you are very social, ENFP is usually an indispensable friend to a selected few, with whom they share their ideals. If you are an ENFP, your friends are very lucky to have you, because the intuitive and emotional nature of your personality enables you to be a perfect empathic mirror to them.

ENFP Romance

For ENFPs, romantic relationships are the center of their world. They approach them very seriously, but also with a childlike joy, enthusiasm and a great amount of energy. They seek deep and truthful relations. For such a connection, they are willing to invest a lot of energy and effort, and always try to make things work. They are loving, caring, intense and have lots of understanding for their partner.

Being an ENFP, you motivate your partner to fulfill all of their dreams and aspirations. Your never-ending optimism is contagious. Although this can be a bit tiring at times for some people, this is still mostly a benefit of being involved with an ENFP. Although you might have a habit of asking "Where did you go, what did you do, how do you feel" sort of questions, it is not because of some insecurity, rather it is for the deep emotional investment.

If you are an ENFP, you have a big heart. This makes you a passionate partner and capable of doing anything that would make your relationship the best it can be. In addition to that, you are an idealist and your values usually bring out the best in people, including your romantic partner. Your empathy and need for a deep relationship, in combination with your need for fun and laughter, creates a strong and rewarding relationship.

You take your commitments very seriously. You are usually very loyal and faithful to your partner – if they prove they are worthy of it. Your personality type respects traditional values. If the relationship is profound, every ENFP will give him/herself completely.

When it comes to sex, you are imaginative, playful and gentle at the same time. Your rich in fantasies and it makes you a creative lover. You always have some new tricks up your sleeve. Being an ENFP you believe, from the bottom of your heart, that sexual intimacy is a positive and amusing way to connect with your partners and show them how deeply you love him/her.

Still, not everything is ideal in relationships with an ENFP. First of all, many of them have a hard time ending a relationship that is not right for them. If you are an ENFP, you usually believe that the fault in a dysfunctional relationship is yours. You consider both success and failure to be solely your responsibility. Your perfectionism makes you a bad loser. Therefore, you tend to stay in a relationship which should have ended long ago. When it is finally over, you still believe it is you who failed, and that there must be something that you could have done to save it.

On the other hand, there is one personality trait that gets in the way of an ENFP's relationship. You frequently lose focus and sometimes cannot stay in a monogamous relationship because of that. You can vividly see all the possibilities out there, and your attention tends to wander off to the green pastures somewhere else. In case your partner is not someone who loves adventures and shares your ideals, you might get easily bored. If you are an ENFP, you know that if you are bored and without a goal ahead of you, you may get very unhappy. It may happen that you end a relationship only to get excitement.

ENFP needs constant reassurance that they are loved. Because of that, they are people who "go hunting" for compliments, and they need to hear from their loved ones that they are appreciated and cared for. They are eager to give back even more, and strive for unconditional love. As warm as they are, they are not selfish, and take a lot of satisfaction in making their partner happy and joyful.

If you are in a relationship with an ENFP you may have a problem on how to express any kind of disapproval, because they are very sensitive to it and believe that every criticism is an attack on their complex personality. Conflicts are a source of enormous stress to them, and they tend to sweep problems under the rug, rather than confront them. They just want the conflict to go away, and can even agree with something they feel strongly against, just to make peace with their partner. But, since they are the ones who stick very firmly to their principles, this just prolongs the disagreement. If you are romantically involved with an ENFP, try reassuring them that the world will not end if they openly disagree with something, and it can even contribute to building a stronger and more profound connection with you. Also, help them accept a critique from you in a more objective way, without inflating it into a huge personal battle and seeing it as an assault to their character.

If you are an ENFP, you are very flexible in all of your relations, as well as your romantic relationships. You get along with most of the other personality types quite well. However, when searching for love, an ideal partner is either an INTJ or INFJ.

7 Actionable Steps for Overcoming Your Weaknesses as an ENFP

Knowing yourself is an essential tool for everyone to improve their quality of life. It is far more pleasant, especially for ENFPs, to read about our strengths, since they perceive every hint of negative feedback as a criticism. But, it is not always like that. Knowing our weak spots make us stronger and better. When we are aware of them, we can take steps to overcome our weaknesses and perfect ourselves.

For an ENFP, it is hard to say what the flaws are. They radiate such positive energy all around themselves, they are loved by the crowd, and they seem to be excited about every new project. So what can be wrong with that? Well, there are the shortcomings that hide behind that bubbly personality which make him/her underperform. If you are an ENFP, here are some actionable steps for you to overcome your weaknesses:

1. Learn to See Things Through

ENFPs tend to be a little bit all over the place. They pick up many projects at once, without much chance to finish them. They are constantly on the run – let's face it, they love the excitement. This can be an adrenalin rush for some time, but most superiors, professors or colleagues will not be too satisfied with that kind of a worker/student. The same applies to personal relationships. If you are an ENFP, you get easily bored and need constant excitement. For that reason, you might even change your romantic partners as soon as they start to seem too familiar. Learn to see many wonderful things that come from this level of relationship, and if the person is right for you, keep pushing forward.

2. Learn to Handle Your Mood Swings

You are an optimist by nature, and you do look at the world through pink glasses. Yet, because you are so extremely open towards everyone, you are prone to tremendous mood swings. You are very empathetic, and you pick up every little change in someone's feelings. In addition to that, you take every critique as an assault to your personality and that makes you become angry or depressed. Since your primary care is to make everyone feel comfortable, you will probably sit on your anger without expressing it. Even suppressed emotions influence our behavior and thinking, and you need to learn to deal with all sorts of feelings so that you do not fall under the destructive effects of suppressing those negative feelings.

3. Take Negative Feedback without Being Insulted

Every hint of negative feedback gets to you in a dramatic way. You tend to feel that the comment refers to your personality, not your work, or some action by itself. The constructive conversation stops and you usually withdraw from that kind of interaction. You may even try to prove excessively that you are worthy, even though the criticism was just a partial comment on your specific behavior. You might feel angry with the person giving you the feedback. This is the sign for you to remember to take that sort of information in a more objective way, not as a personal attack on your entire personality.

4. Stay Away from Those Who Dislike to Display Affection

You have a warm, loving nature. You believe that public and/or intensive display of affection is what everyone needs to feel good. You love someone and they should see it in everything you do. You also need constant reassurance that you are loved back. But, not all personality types are comfortable with this, even though they have strong feelings for someone. You need to take that into account so you do not feel hurt if you are in a relationship with such a person.

5. Prepare Yourself for Negative Outcomes

You are not supposed to stop being such a positive and contagious optimist. The fact is, not everything goes as planned, and people do not always have good intentions. This is why it is good for you to be aware of the possibility that something might go wrong, and have some solutions at hand. That way, you will not get completely caught by surprise – at work or in personal relationships.

6. Use Objective Assessments to Make Decisions

You look at the world through one (your) perspective. This is typical for all people, but in your case it is more prominent than most other personality types. Your enormous capacity to feel has a downside – you perceive everything to be connected to you and take things subjectively. But, when making any life decisions, try to look at it more objectively. Try to ask your friends to help you with that initially, sharing their take on things with you.

7. Focus on Details of the Project

You absolutely hate anything that even resembles routine, rules, or dull activities. This makes you fun and an exciting person, but, on the other hand, it may cause you to lose jobs, miss deadlines, leave a white picket fence project around your house incomplete, etc. You do not need to go against your nature and try to become a stereotype, but learn how to find something interesting and stimulating even in the details of the work. Ultimately, that will help you finish what you have started.

The 10 Most Influential ENFPs We Can Learn From

There are not too many ENFPs in this world. It is estimated that between 3 and 5 percent of us have preference for Extroversion, Intuition, Feeling and Perceiving. Nevertheless, even this small number of people has tremendous influence on mankind. Their philanthropy, optimism and pro-activeness make the difference in this world. They are often found in politics, movie or music industry, arts, and from these positions, they are trying to spread the message of belief in people.

Here are some of the influential ENFPs and their accomplishments:

1. George Orson Welles

George Orson Welles was an American Actor, director, writer and producer. He is known for his most innovative work in theater, radio and film. He is also famous for pushing the boundaries, especially with the 1938. Radio broadcast "The War of the Worlds", was probably the most famous broadcast in the radio history. *Citizen Kane* was his first film, and is ranked as one of greatest hits of all-time. It may also be seen as an artist's personal struggle with difficulties of being a "people person" and a need to back away from the society.

2. Bob Dylan

Bob Dylan is an American singer, songwriter and a writer. Most of his success dates back to his work in the 1960s, which interpreted political and social issues. This made him a real "man of the people". Dylan is also one of the best-selling artists of all time. In May 2012, Dylan received The Presidential Medal of Freedom from Barack Obama.

3. William Oliver Stone

William Oliver Stone is an American producer, screenwriter, film director, and also a military veteran. Many of his movies have controversial political and cultural issues as a theme. His ability to interpret situations shows his knowledge of how a person's mind works. He was a signatory of the third Humanist Manifesto.

4. Walter Elias "Walt Disney

Walter Elias "Walt" Disney created numerous cartoon characters, including Mickey Mouse, Donald Duck and Goofy. He was well known for his innovative personality. He managed to breathe life into his characters by investing all of his creativity. He is a perfect example that ENFP's enthusiasm makes him stop being realistic. A fascinating number of fictional characters also speak about the ENFPs' characteristic of getting easily bored.

5. Aldous Leonard Huxley

Aldous Leonard Huxley was an English writer and a philosopher. He was best known for his novel *Brave New World*. Huxley was a pacifist, humanist and a satire writer. Judging by his biography and his work, he is definitely a perfect fit as an ENFP. Huxley suffered from an illness (keratitis punctata), which left him practically blind for a few years. That did not prevent him from applying to the army in World War I. He was declined on medicinal grounds, but the decision itself testifies about his determination and his personality. After recovering from his illness, he studied English literature, and that is more than a proof of his indestructible optimism. His science fiction novel *Brave New World* confirms his futuristic, visionary and innovative tendencies, as well as his immaculate perception of others' motives and thoughts.

6. Timothy Walter "Tim" Burton

Timothy Walter "Tim" Burton is an American film director, producer, artist, writer and animator. He is an all-around artist whose work is always original and new. He wrote and illustrated a poetry book called *The Melancholy Death of Oyster Boy & Other Stories*. His imagination is inspiring, and people who worked with him had only words of praise for him. He is an example of the diversity that is typical for ENFPs. His mind works constantly on the border of fantasy, but you can see that he has intense understanding of human psyche as well.

7. Charles John Huffam Dickens

Charles John Huffam Dickens was an English writer and a social critic. He is widely popular, and his fictional characters show an immense ability to observe different personalities, their ways and society as a whole. His work challenges everyone to be better and more sensitive to the differences between us.

8. Mark Twain

Mark Twain was an American writer mostly known for his novel *Adventures of Tom Sawyer* and *Adventures of Huckleberry Finn.* His work shows us the eternally childish and playful nature of an ENFP. His references to slavery demonstrate his philanthropic spirit as well.

9. Robin McLaurin Williams

Robin McLaurin Williams was an American actor and a comedian. He was known for his improvisational skills, and he was a great example of ENFPs' ability to make people around him feel good, make them laugh and inspire them for greatness. As well as many other ENFPs, he had prominent philanthropic values, and had done a lot to contribute to different causes. He also had a history of a pursuit for an ideal life partner and was looking for an intense connection with a significant other. He had also cherished family values and was a wonderful, yet playful, father to his children.

10. Meg Ryan

Meg Ryan is an American actress and a film producer. She played the leading roles in several romantic-comedy films, including *Sleepless in Seattle.* Her sensibility shines through her roles, and she is both entertaining and insightful. Like most ENFPs, she is not only an artist; she has a need to give back. She is politically active, and has supported the Democratic Party, especially its environmental protection programs and initiatives.

There are many more famous ENFPs, and there is a lot to learn from all of them – how to love intensely, be joyful, contribute to causes and treat everyone with respect.

Conclusion

A person with preferences for Extroversion Intuition Feeling and Perceiving is a unique and cherished person. He or she is one of the rare. Charisma, optimism and genuine care for people, are the traits that make an ENFP the one who definitely does not go through life unnoticed.

If you are an ENFP, you are probably well aware of all of your strengths. You know that you are good at dealing with unexpected challenges and situations. You also know that you thrive when all limits are pushed aside, and you have a chance of testing both yourself and the established ways of doing things. You are aware of the fact that almost everybody you meet likes you. It is not arrogant to say that you change people's lives. You encourage people to better themselves in every possible way. You bring joy and liveliness to every group. Your enthusiasm gives wings to every venture. You strive for ultimate authenticity. You need your relationships to be meaningful and deep.

It is now your mission to do for yourself what you might easily do for others – that is, to inspire yourself to perfection.

In order to do so, you also need to be aware of your weaknesses. Not just be conscious of them, but also work to overcome them. Firstly, this means you will not withdraw from looking your flaws in the eye. Secondly, you must not to take the advice as a personal insult. This is one of your weak points. Be mindful of your tendency to leave things unfinished as soon as they start to appear uninteresting to you. Try and find new aspects of the same work, project, person, or relationship. This will help you stay focused and motivated, and keep a good job, or a compatible partner. This way, no one will get hurt and you will not torment yourself feeling that it was you who needed to make everything work. In addition to that, keep in mind that if a relationship does not work it is not simply because it is becoming known and familiar to you, but because you and your partner are not a good fit for each other. You have a tendency to stay in a relationship that is dysfunctional for far too long. Think about it, and do not waste anybody's precious time.

The road ahead is indeed exciting, full of adventures and accomplishments. You are a kind of person that can achieve miracles. You are committed to your values, you are loving and caring, an altruist, capable, intelligent, a visionary; and most of all – brave enough to make a change in the world!

Final Word/About the Author

I was born and raised in Norwalk, Connecticut. Growing up, I could often be found spending afternoons reading in the local public library about management techniques and leadership styles, along with overall outlooks towards life. It was from spending those afternoons reading about how others have led productive lives that I was inspired to start studying patterns of human behavior and self-improvement. Usually I write works around sports to learn more about influential athletes in the hopes that from my writing, you the reader can walk away inspired to put in an equal if not greater amount of hard work and perseverance to pursue your goals. However, I began writing about psychology topics such as the Myers Brigg Type Indicator so that I could help others better understand why they act and think the way they do and how to build on their strengths while also identifying their weaknesses. If you enjoyed

ENFP: Understanding & Relating with the Champion please leave a review! Also, you can read more of my works on *INFPs, ENFJs, ISFPs, ISFJs, ESFJs, ESTJs, How to be Witty, How to be Likeable, How to be Creative, Bargain Shopping, Productivity Hacks, Morning Meditation, Becoming a Father,* and *33 Life Lessons: Success Principles, Career Advice & Habits of Successful People* in the Kindle Store.

Like what you read?

If you love books on life, basketball, or productivity, check out my website at claytongeoffreys.com to join my exclusive list where I let you know about my latest books. Aside from being the first to hear about my latest releases, you can also download a free copy of *33 Life Lessons: Success Principles, Career Advice & Habits of Successful People.* See you there!

Made in the USA
Lexington, KY
11 December 2015